HBF

HELPFUL BOOK FOR

BUSINESSPERSON

How to Start a Successful Restaurant Business

Things to Consider Before Opening a Restaurant Business

HBF
EDITORIAL

HOW TO START A SUCCESSFUL RESTAURANT BUSINESS
Things to Consider Before Opening a Restaurant Business

© H.B.F. Editorial, 2014
© George F. Howard
   Master Resell Rights

ISBN-13: 978-1502553652
ISBN-10: 1502553651

Table of Contents

What do you know about running a restaurant?

Things to Note in Running a Restaurant

Having your own restaurant is one of the most fulfilling and enjoyable business ventures. Food is a renewable commodity. This means that people won't stop looking for different sources of food because dining out is entertaining as well as functional.

Many people dream of owning their own restaurants, whether it is fast food, coffee shops or gourmet. In reality, many people fail to sustain their restaurants and most of them die during their first year of operation. This is due to the lack of preparation and dedication on the part of the owner. Many people jump into the industry too fast without really weighing the pro's and con's of the project or having the necessary expertise.

However, there is a way to lessen the risk that is associated with new ventures such as restaurants. Preventive planning and proper management are keys towards success but there are also small things which count in the whole process of owning a restaurant.

Every business needs a business plan. Business plans are meant to lay down the different conditions and characteristics that should be inherent in the business. The availability of a good business plan which has been carefully formulated is a step towards success.

You will find information about creating a business plan in an upcoming chapter, however, some points to consider are :

Crystal clear description of the concept of the restaurant

The objective and the general description of the concept of the restaurant need to be specific. This will give a general overview of what the restaurant intends to do and for whom it intends to do it. The concept of the restaurant needs to be established because it is the core idea by which everything else will follow.

There are many things to be considered in designing the overall concept of the restaurant (excluding food) such as:

What type of restaurant do you want?

What special features would it have which would set it aside from all the other similar restaurants in town? What's the overall selling factor of the restaurant?

Target market

The restaurant's target market needs to be identified. No single restaurant should try to aim at targeting all kinds of people. Even fast food restaurants have a specific target market, even though it may seem at first that it caters to people of all walks of life.
The concept of the restaurant needs to be aligned with the target market. The target market will depend on the owner of the restaurant, and the selection can be based on the type of food or even the personal preference of the owner.

Food category, food items and their prices

Before starting a restaurant or even before entertaining the thought of opening up a restaurant, the kind of food to be served is usually identified first.

Most owners put up restaurants according to their favorite kind of food. There are also restaurants which are inspired by one-time experiences such as eating excellent foreign foods. There are many choices that are available for aspiring restaurant owners. The details of the food category should be identified next. The specific items in the menu should also be identifie. Of course, the pricing of these items is very important for it will determine the feasibility of the business.

Financial evaluation

After the prices of the food items have been determined, it's time to develop the financials of the project. You can hire a professional consultant in determining the financial viability of the restaurant. All the project costs and risks should be included in the business plan.

Ownership

An enthusiast may consider creating a small corporation or a partnership or a single proprietorship to be able to give the restaurant a legal entity. You should check the local requirements for creating such institutions

Marketing plan

Include a marketing plan because it is integral to the success of the restaurant.

There are so many other things that should be considered before entering into the restaurant business. The ones listed above are only part of the whole scheme of restaurant creation. The most important thing is that the restaurant should reflect the preferences of the owner so as to make it enjoyable. However, a lot of thought should be given to the way it's going to generate money because this is the only way that the restaurant will become sustainable.

We have covered some of the important information about having a business plan. This subject, as well as other relevant planning information is covered in depth in upcoming chapters.

What kind of restaurant do you want to own?

Different Types of Restaurants

Entrepreneurs who are thinking about starting their own restaurants should realize that restaurants are generally seen as good business ventures. Why? Because people are always looking for food.

There are different types of restaurants that businessmen can look into starting up and the decision regarding what type of restaurant or what style to put up is based on different factors.

The decision regarding the general concept of a restaurant business will be dependent on different major things. Listed below are some of these factors:

Location

The style of the restaurant will be dependent on the location. For example, if someone is thinking about putting up a Chinese-style restaurant in a place where there are many types of Chinese Restaurants, he might want to tweak some details about his restaurant to be able to have a competitive advantage against the other Chinese restaurants in the area. Perhaps he would stick with the general concept of having a Chinese restaurant because the place is popular for this type of food but he might want to add different types of cuisine as well, perhaps go into fusion cooking.

Be sure and read Chapter 15 on location.

- Target Market

The target market is very important in determining what style of restaurant to put up. A busy place where class B society thrives may be an optimum location to put up a mid-scale fast food restaurant.

Different restaurants cater to different types of people and no one restaurant aims at capturing the whole of the market because it would just end up in confusion.

- Availability of Materials

The budding restaurateur might want to look closely at the availability of the materials in the area. For example, a seafood restaurant will depend greatly on the availability of fresh ingredients and seafood in the local market. If not, the owner will have to look for other alternatives which can cost him additional money.

- Availability of good cooks

There are more than enough restaurants in many areas today. The only thing that separates the good ones from the average is the type of cooks. The style of the restaurant should match the skills of the hired chef. There are good chefs who can easily adjust to styles which they aren't really accommodated with but these chefs are very hard to find and perhaps, they will ask for a very hefty salary.

- Personal Preference

Of course, every business is built upon vision and the personal preference of the owner will ultimately determine the style of restaurant that he will start. There are ways to beat the normal odds which go against the success of new restaurants.

There are a lot of different styles of restaurants which one can choose from. These are:

- Steakhouses

These restaurants usually cater to the middle and upper class markets. These are also usually oriented towards families and have a very relaxed and homey atmosphere. The meals in steakhouses are usually deemed as good buys. There are also the high-end steakhouses which concentrate more on the quality of the meat which they serve.

- Seafood Restaurants

There are different types of seafood restaurants. There are the quick-service ones, the ones which cater to the middle class and the higher-end ones which cater to the upper class. The quick service seafood restaurants are very much similar to fast-food restaurants. Generally, seafood restaurants offer a wide variety of seafood and they serve it in different fashions.

- Casual Dining

This type of restaurant caters to almost all kinds of people. People go here to be able to have a lot of food choices and enjoy the relaxed kind of atmosphere. The prices in casual dining restaurants are usually not that high.

- Pizzeria

There are basically two choices in creating a pizzeria. The first one is to construct a full-blown restaurant which doesn't only serve pizza but many different kinds of Italian food as well. The other choice is to specialize in pizzas and a few other items such as beer.

- Coffeehouse

More and more people are being enticed to go to coffeehouses. These coffeehouses offer the coziest atmospheres for small talk and coffee conversations.

These are only a few of the choices that you have in developing a concept for your restaurant. Explore other choices and stick with the one which satisfies the heart most.

How will you design your restaurant?

A Good Design

A good design and layout plan are necessary for having a good restaurant. Restaurants are good businesses which can be very fulfilling. The mere fact that people go to your restaurant to eat is already something to cherish. It's like having people inside your home every once in a while craving your home-baked goodies.

A successful restaurant will need a good design and layout plan. Design and layout plans are dependent on different factors which will influence the final decisions later on.

In fact, the output of the layout plans can definitely affect the success of the restaurant. People often go to a new restaurant and they think to themselves "they should have put that plant elsewhere, it obstructs the good view" or "I wish they hadn't put too much light in here." These are small things which can really add up and end up influencing the customers to go to the other side of the street where another restaurant is calling out to their taste buds. After the type of food and service are identified, the next step is to hire consultants regarding the design of the restaurant. These are some of the things that you need to take into consideration when considering different floor and layout plans for the restaurant.

Density of customers

The layout plan should be based mostly on the comfort of the patrons. Even fast food restaurants consider the density of people, especially in peak hours, even though it may seem that these restaurants become too crowded during lunch time.

For formal dining restaurants which cater to the upper class income, it may be wise to provide more space between the tables since these restaurants don't really rely on the number of people per day. Their revenues depend on the pricing of the food items. There should be more provision for eye candy such as furniture and art works.

Style of service

The layout and floor plans should also be based on the type of service that the restaurant will give. Fast food restaurants and self-service restaurants would need less distance between the tables since the food won't be served there. For other restaurants which provide table service, the space between the tables is very important so as to prevent too much clutter from happening in a specific part of the restaurant.

Type of building

The layout plan is restricted by the type of structure where the restaurant will be built. You should be able to take into consideration all the different curves and the minor details in the structure before proceeding.

Lighting

Proper lighting is very important for every restaurant. The lighting should be able to match the mood and the type of service of the restaurant. A relaxed atmosphere can be complemented by bright lighting while serene and serious moods can be accompanied by subtler shades.

Designing the restaurant will be divided into two important parts: the dining area and the production area.

The dining area is important because this is the essence of the structure of the restaurant. The people should be comfortable in eating in the restaurant and this will be determined as early as the designing phase. Studies have revealed that 50 percent of the time, people come in restaurants as pairs, 30 percent come alone while the remaining 20 percent usually come in groups.

The production area is the second major part of any restaurant. The main thing about the production area should be efficiency. The organization of the kitchen will determine the speed by which the food can be cooked and served. The production area design should take into consideration other things like space for storage, food preparation, baking, cooking, trash storage, production aisles, employee facilities and other such matters.

In hiring design consultants, the restaurant owner should always remember to put a clause of confidentiality in the contract. This is to prevent the consultants from leaking certain parts of the design to other people, especially to the competitors. This can be as simple as a single-line clause which states that everything regarding the design will be owned by the client.

These are some useful things to remember in designing your restaurant. The most important thing to remember is the people who will be eating at the restaurant for they will be the ultimate lever of its success or failure.

Startup costs that can't be overlooked

Know Your Restaurant's Start up Cost

The cost of opening your own restaurant business is one very important matter to be dealt with and often the hardest to determine because, to a great extent, it depends on the type of restaurant that you desire to open.

Your restaurant "start-up costs" are outlined as expenses incurred for the acquisition or creation of your restaurant business. "Start-up costs" are comprised as any incurred amounts or out-going capital in relation with your restaurant's activity directed for income generation before your restaurant business starts.

"Start-up costs" generally include the following expenses:

- Potential markets surveys.
- Evaluation of available supplies, labor, facilities, etc.
- Advertisements.
- Business equipment and fixtures.
- Equipment and fixture installation.
- Decorating and remodeling.
- Employee uniforms.
- Salaries for employees undergoing training and their trainers.
- Costs of travel for acquiring prospective suppliers, distributors or customers.
- Fees and salaries for consultants and executives and other similar services.

Estimating your restaurant business' "start up costs":

It is a wise decision to study your "start-up costs" estimate with a qualified accountant.

1. Begin by recording then add up your entire restaurant's equipment which you consider is necessary to begin and manage your restaurant. See the chapter on selecting equipment and furnishings for more help on this.
2. On your list, mark off certain items or equipment that aren't really necessary and can wait.

Determine what kind of equipment needs to be bought brand new, and what type can be purchased used.

1. Determine what things may be leased, for the moment.

2. When adding up the physical cost (building or office) of your restaurant, remember to also add in the remodeling costs, decorating costs, fixtures, installation and delivery fees for equipment and fixtures.

3. Include professional fees, utility deposits, permits and licenses.

4. When computing your advertising costs, make sure to add trademarks, logo expenses as well as other graphics to be used.

5. Come up with ways where you may be able to lower some expenses. Call vendors and suppliers and work out certain deals.

6. Estimate that all expenses will be much higher than expected. It is sensible to add about 1-5 percent to your estimate.

7. Write your business plan before you come to your final estimate for "start up costs". Generally, a business plan functions to reveal more "start-up costs" that weren't really thought of. Again, see the chapter on preparing your business plan.

8. Include your restaurant's first 3-6 months operating investment in your "start-up costs". These expenses will usually include employee salaries, advertising, rent, supplies, delivery expenses, utilities, taxes, insurance, maintenance, professional services, loan payments, inventory, etc.

Before opening your restaurant:

1. Work in or volunteer in a similar restaurant like the one you want to open. In doing this, you will be able to menu development, restaurant marketing, payroll and many other important elements of the food business.

2. Determine your "target market". What type of crowd do you want to cater? Is it teenagers, family or seniors? Determining your target customers before you begin planning will help you organize your menu and will help establish your décor, atmosphere and location of your business.

3. Pick out a food concept and style of service. Generally, your service style can be fast-food, offering fries, burgers, sandwiches and hotdogs; mid-scale offering value-priced full "course meals"; or upscale, providing high-class ambiance with "full service meals" with higher prices.

4. Develop your business plan. Again, see the chapter on preparing your business plan but make sure the plan includes:

    • Your restaurant's general concept and objective;
    • Detailed financial projections and information; your menu and pricing;
    • Employee and equipment details;
    • Marketing and advertising plan;
    • Possible exit strategy.

5. Create your menu. Know that your menu can either "make or break" your restaurant, therefore it must be in conformity with your restaurant's overall concept. We have devoted an entire chapter to creating your menu.

6. Choose your location. Look for a location where there is a continuous flow of traffic, accessible parking, and near or along other businesses. The chapter on location will be helpful.

7. Know restaurant safety regulations. Typically, restaurants are controlled and are subject to inspection. You must know the local regulations and conform to them.

8. Hire your employees. Make certain that your employment announcements specifically declare your specified requirements.

Starting a restaurant business has its challenges and also its rewards. Before starting any business, research first. Make sure you are suited for entrepreneurship as well as recognize that there is significant effort required. Therefore, it is necessary that you enjoy whatever you are venturing into as well as you have confidence in your service or product because it will consume most of your important time, especially when it is still beginning.

How to advertise the restaurant

Advertising Your Restaurant Effectively: Advertising or Public Relations?

Positive public recognition is important for your restaurant's success; this recognition can be accomplished through "public relations campaign" as well as advertising.

Note that a "public relations campaign" and advertising are two very different things. Both are meant to elevate the interest of consumers in a service or product and both use generally the same tools, like radio, television, print and the internet, advertising uses ads and public relations uses news.

Here is a look at advertising and public relations differences:

1.   Message control

As to how, where and when an advertisement flows, is very controllable. An ad space bought in the correct format like radio, broadcast, online, print, etc. implies that you have control over the messages that you want to communicate.

On the other hand, while the message creating process by means of public relations is also very controllable, it is what happens or results after your message has departed is usually uncontrollable, which brings up the question of whether potential customers perceive the information you supplied as newsworthy. In public relations, it makes sure it is.

2.   Information Personalization

Advertisements, being very costly, don't provide you with enough room to customize or personalize your restaurant's story.

A public relations promotion does this, by creating a story of multiple angles aimed to successfully reach various media outlets like daily newspapers, business journals, food service publications, city magazines, entertainment and dining publications, national magazines, etc. You increase your broadcast and reach more audiences that will be educated about your restaurant.

3.   Implied Endorsement

In advertising, you pay somebody to have your message directly filtered to your prospect consumers.

With public relations however, it can afford the reliability of an indirect endorsement of a "third-party". Meaning you don't pay to get advertised, publications offered to you for free, granting you space so you can rely your restaurant's story to customers. This endorsement is an efficient tool in sculpting public opinion.

4.   Cost-Effectiveness

There can be no comparison to the "cost" of display advertising in a magazine or publication as to the "cost" of distributing and writing an informative press release.
Hiring a firm to create press releases for your restaurant is definitely many times cheaper compared to advertising costs.

Furthermore, press release articles are viewed by more audiences since consumers are more interested in stories as opposed to advertisements.

5.   Life Span

With public relations, a well-constructed story can have the attention of the reader for a long time, where an ad is noticed by the viewer in a span of just about 5 minutes.

Consumers normally clip certain articles they read, such as a new destination that they would want to visit or a new restaurant where they would want to sample food.

The goal of public relations is to maintain a "noise" or sort of an ongoing talk about your restaurant and what it has to offer, and build up credibility. There are many media outlets that you can easily reach when you have made a "well-expressed" plan as well as the appropriate public relations company to execute it.

So when will you be using public relations? Why and when to advertise? The answer lies with you and you alone. It all depends on your needs and on what you want to accomplish. You can use both advertising and public relations as your marketing tools together, or separately as the situation demands.

Market analysis

Market Analysis: How to Keep Your Focus in the Restaurant Business

The food service industry caters to a universal need of humans – to be nourished. However, the way food appeals to humans isn't at all universal. Mankind is a diverse group and there isn't one particular operation of food service that could satisfy this diversity.

This is one reality that aspirants in the restaurant business find difficulty to accept. Many hopefuls think they can catch everyone, but such efforts end up in failure. They neglect to consider that trying to cater to everyone results into not being able to cater to anyone at all.

It is best to just concentrate on a small part of the market, say ten percent or so, this way, you can offer the best service for that part of your choice. This is done by doing a market analysis – the study of the potential target market.

The senior market is composed of people who are 65 years or older. Seniors generally live on fixed incomes, from their pension or sustenance by relatives, and thus have a rather inflexible spending power. Most seniors usually go to family-oriented eating places such as lunch buffets because they offer good food and services at affordable prizes. Less active seniors usually prefer smaller portions as they may have smaller appetites.

When targeting seniors, it is best to make them special by offering senior promotions, or lowered rates. You can also market your restaurant as senior-friendly by emphasizing safety features such as ramps and handlebars.

The late adult market is composed of people aged 50 to 64. They are usually the ones who are experiencing the empty nest syndrome, where grownup children have left the home. This market usually has the most stable financial status as they could be in the most advanced stages in their careers. At this point, price usually doesn't matter. This is the age when people start trying to really enjoy life and its pleasures. So the main concern is good food and service. When targeting this market, it is good to present your restaurant with elegance and sophistication. It would be wise to invest more on ambience and class.

The middle aged group is composed of people who are around 40 to 50 years old. These are very productive years as most executives and prominent career people fall in this market. Money is rather plentiful and thus spent with more generosity. In this age, people are quite fond of trendy and high-end, fine dining restaurants. Many people in this market already have grandchildren and thus this is also good for family-friendly eating places which that are more formal than those frequented by the senior market.

The young adult market consists of people in their mid twenties to just before reaching middle age. This is an age of great effort for established families. The main concern here is enjoying children and keeping a good relationship with them. People belonging in this market usually look for eating places that are conducive for bonding with their children. Places that offer food fast, and with bigger quantities such as family brunch buffet restaurants which are big hits for this market. It is important to offer comfort and a laid-back ambience for this type of market.

The young market comprises of those in their early twenties and younger. This is probably the most diverse market. The main concern of people in this market is instant gratification with low prices. This is the primary market for the fast food industry. A good strategy for this target market is keeping updated with the latest trends and offering food services in association to what is "cool" and "hip".

Cash, check or charge?

How Best to Collect the Tons of Money You Will Earn with Your New Restaurant – Cash, Check or Charge?

Perhaps the most exciting part when establishing a restaurant, or any business for that matter, is collecting the money. What is business for but to earn? For some the only concern is the money. Money these days is no longer limited to a single monetary form but different modes as well, which may be called the three big C's – cash, check, and card or charge. Which is the best mode to earn? This could be a puzzling question for the aspiring entrepreneur. Hopefully, the following will help clear things up.

Cash: Instant Gratification

Perhaps the most common form of money is cash. Nothing wets the appetite for business like crisp new bills. It is the monetary form you are most familiar with and thus, the one most connected to profits and earnings. Cash is good, because it is money in its clearest form, tangible and physical, it is finance incarnate. It is immediately disposable and can be used anywhere.

However, more people try to avoid carrying cash nowadays. First, cash can be bulky; carrying a lot entails one to bring wads of paper. Second, since cash is physical money, it is very risky and can be lost. Once it is gone, there's practically now way of retrieving it. It can easily be stolen and can even lure danger by attracting robbers and other bad elements. It can be dangerous to customers as they can easily be held up. It can be dangerous to restaurateurs as well because it can it can be easily be embezzled. While cash can give instant gratification, great security is needed to ensure its preservation.

Check: Symbolic Cash
Checks can be very useful for people who have money in the bank. With checks, you can still spend money without having to carry thick bundles of paper around. Checks can be quite secure as the money it represents can only be claimed by the intended recipient, unless of course if the check is written paid to cash.

There are many advantages in using checks, but there are also drawbacks that could inconvenience the recipient. Checks need to be cashed, which takes time and extra effort for the collector. The money collected can't be spent immediately. Checks expire after a few months, usually six. Perhaps the greatest danger that checks may entail are insufficient funds. The customer paying with a check may not have enough money in their account. It takes more time and effort to gain the money being earned.

Charge: A Promise to Be Redeemed

Plastic money or the credit card is now growing as the most popular form of monetary exchange. It is convenient and easy to use. It is easy to carry and has a lot of spending power in a small package. Consumers love using it because of the extra perks that come with it, such as airline miles and bonus gifts. On the recipient's end, money collection is certain, since the responsibility of payment belongs to the credit card company, who carries the burden of chasing delinquent customers as well. The payments may also be directly credited to the recipient's bank account, making the sale secure.

Convenient as it may be, credit cards aren't devoid of disadvantages. Credit card companies usually charge significant percentages of sales and could diminish your earnings. Money can also take time to collect and there is more paperwork needed to claim money. Credit card fraud is very possible and can victimize both customers and restaurant owners.

Perhaps the best alternative of all is the debit card. The debit card represents everything good about cash with none of the headaches of checks. A debit card purchase is like having instant cash. A debit card looks like a credit card but functions like a check or cash. When a customer presents a debit card, the merchant swipes the card just like a credit card. The checking account of the presenter is queried to determine if there are sufficient funds in the account to cover the purchase and the amount is immediately deducted and transferred to the merchants account. This is definitely the next best thing to cash!

The Final Verdict

In choosing which mode of payment is best for one's restaurant the final choice boils down to the customer. Restaurateurs should keep in mind what mode is best for customers to pay – what is most convenient to them with regards to their profile. It might not be advisable for a place that caters to children and teens to accept only credit cards since most kids don't have cards yet. It might not be advisable to refuse checks or credit cards for fine dining that caters to executives, as prices would be high and bring lots of cash that could be very inconvenient and secure. Of course it is good to have all modes available.

With careful study of the benefits of each mode of payment alongside the market profile, an aspiring restaurateur may be able to choose the best payment option for their restaurant. Hopefully money will rake in by the bundles, whether in cash, check, or charge.

How to write your menu

The Art of Menu Writing – the Secret to the Overall Success of any Restaurant

Among the most consistent fixtures in any decent restaurant are the menus. They are one of the first things that greet you when you enter your favorite eating place as they are usually posted at the entrance or immediately handed to you once you are seated. You read them, use them, and then totally forget about them once the waiter has taken your order.

But menus do more than just list what a restaurant can offer. The menu is important to the overall success of the restaurant. Everything in a restaurant's operation is linked to the menu and is why it is a very important matter to work on when running a restaurant. No matter how mundane menus may seem to the layman, writing them properly takes effort.

The writing of the menu doesn't begin with the actual writing of what the restaurant can serve, but starts way before that. The art of menu writing begins with the conception of the restaurant. At the restaurant's inception, a theme should be set and this theme should emanate through all the elements of the eating place. Hodgepodge doesn't really work, while fusion may.

Whether it is Italian, Japanese, Chinese, modern or homey, there should be a theme that will stand for the identity of the restaurant. This theme will govern what is inside the menu, from its first print throughout all updates in the future. Having the theme helps narrow down the menu, keeping it simple not only for the customer's eyes but also for the restaurant's inventory. The theme will tell the owner or the chef what not to write in the menu and at the same time it will give the chef an idea of what to include.

After establishing the restaurant's theme and listing the possible items to include in the menu, the next step is for the chef to write down the recipes of the "candidate" items. While the recipes seem not to concern the menu, it is very much connected as the operations in the kitchen are triggered by the customer's orders, which are based on the menu. The recipes will serve as important definitions of what is written on the menu. The recipes are crucial to deliver the items in the menu as consistently as possible. If the chef can't translate the recipe of a particular item simply enough for the cooks to replicate, then it is best to discard the item from the menu no matter how good it may be. Only after the recipes have been written down can the menu be drafted.

After writing the recipe and making the menu draft, the next step is to contact suppliers that provide the ingredients. The chef may be able to produce recipes and a menu of delectable pieces, but they can't be made and served if there are no ingredients. The chef and the owner should be able to source out the items carefully and thoroughly. It is best to contact several suppliers to find one that can give the best quality, most consistent quantity, and most reasonable prices.

This stage in menu writing also determines the prices of the food to be served. The costs of ingredients directly affect the price of the finished dishes. At this point it may be necessary for the chef to substitute certain ingredients that might be too expensive to sell at a reasonable price, or in worse cases, discard a dish totally because the cost might make it impossible to be served.

When a good deal with suppliers has been made, the next crucial step is to test the menu. The chef has to assemble the menu, and then present it to the whole restaurant – the busboys, the waiters, the maitre d', the managers, the owners, and everybody else involved in the service. This will acquaint the whole restaurant to the food and at the same time will help evaluate if the food will be good to serve. At this point it is wise to take pictures of the dishes to serve as a guide for the staff so that they will know how the finished dishes should appear. At the end of the tasting the chef will know if there are necessary changes to be made in the menu. After which, the menu can be finalized.

The last step will be the actual printing of the menus. There are several menu suppliers that will be able to present several types of menus and materials for the restaurant managers to choose from. You may choose a booklet type of menu, or a single paged one. The options are endless. Restaurateurs may choose to outsource the printing of menus or they may opt to invest in a menu printer themselves should they deem it necessary to change the menu more often the usual.

The menu may be just a sheet or some sheets of paper; however it is a very important backbone of a successful restaurant. The steps to write a menu may be tedious, but the efforts to make one are definitely worth it.

How to select the equipment and furnishings

Very Useful Tips on Furnishing Your New Restaurant

Many people dream of setting up their own restaurant and making it big on the culinary scene. However, most of these dreamers stumble and fall because they don't know what it takes to have a decent dining place. A good theme, efficient staff, and reasonable prices are usually planned however one important thing may be overlooked – acquiring equipment and furnishings. Here are some helpful hints for equipping your restaurant.

The first thing to do when looking for restaurant equipment is to know what is needed in a restaurant. The industrial kitchen is so much more complex than the one at home as food is prepared several times more than just three meals a day. Creating a restaurant kitchen is very crucial; you might consider hiring an expert for this, but if you don't have enough funds you can still make it by carefully planning what to get.

As a general rule, restaurant equipment and machines have to be simple, doing only what they are expected. Those with special features more often than not have useless functions that are just included to increase their price. Complicated machines also could result in complicated malfunctions. You only need an oven that bakes, broils, or roasts, not so much one that tells you the time or buzzes when there is a burglar. It is also unwise to buy equipment that has combined functions of usually separate machines. If one of the functions breaks down, more likely, the other functions will also, thus debilitating your kitchen two or three times more.

Acquiring restaurant equipment doesn't necessarily mean buying. You usually have the option to lease or rent equipment. Leasing is useful for those who don't have enough finances to purchase all equipment. Leasing also lets the owner pay for the equipment only when it is needed to be used. The option of getting newer equipment is more realistic with leasing; you can always get a new replacement piece after the lease of the previous one expires.

Major maintenance of the equipment is also the responsibility of the owner, which frees you of costs of fixing broken equipment. The drawback with leasing is that it can be rather expensive in the long run, but if you are earning a lot, then its advantages might be worth it. Some pieces of equipment that are advisable to lease are coffeemakers, ice machines, dish washers, and linens. Coffee machines can be acquired for free from companies that sell the coffee, so long as you keep buying your beans from them. Ice machines can burn out easily and is advisable to lease to prevent the hassle of constant repairs. Dish washers are quite expensive and leasing may be a good solution to acquire them, and like with coffee companies, some detergent manufacturers lend dish washers to loyal customers. Linens can also be leased, and usually the lease includes laundering, delivery, and storage.

New equipment can be quite expensive, but who says you have to buy all new equipment. There are several used restaurant equipment stores that could serve their purpose well but cost several times less than brand new gear. You just have to make sure that there is assurance from the seller that the equipment will work, at least for a while. Dispensable pieces like knobs and nuts are okay not to be in perfect condition since you can replace them anyway. What matters is the general performance of the machine. It should be able to work a reasonable amount of time where you can still earn enough at least to buy new equipment when the old one finally conks out. Among the equipments that are fine to buy second hand are gas ranges, fryers, ovens, grills, and tools such as tongs and mashers. They are generally simple equipment that last long enough for a second owner to use decently.

Buying equipment is one of the most crucial components of establishing a restaurant. With careful planning, you can make the most of your equipment, with the most affordable costs to you.

Hiring your staff

Hiring the Best Staff for Your Restaurant

The food service industry is one that involves a lot of personal relations. Hiring a good staff is one of the most crucial steps when starting your restaurant. It could make or break a restaurant, no matter how good the ambience, the facilities, or the location. The recruitment process in a restaurant is very tedious but fortunately human resource practitioners have provided tips that can help in hiring a good restaurant staff.

The recruitment process for a restaurant doesn't start with the actual interview or even the posting of job advertisements. It begins with knowing what it is that the restaurant owner wants the staff to do. Having a general knowledge of what tasks are required of the crew helps create the job description which is crucial for advertising the job vacancy and for sifting through the pool of applicants. The job description need not to be too formal but it has to state in a clear manner the responsibilities of the position. They should also list important required credentials and skills that the applicants should have to at least be considered.

The next thing to do is devise a payment scheme. The services your potential employees will give you should be compensated accordingly. It is important to research the salary ranges in your area. For each position, you should set a range of salary because the pay also depends on the workers. It is important to match the salary with the qualification of those you hire. Take into consideration the inclusion of tips for certain jobs.

It is also important for you to create an application form. Applicants should provide you the information you need to know about them before you interview and hire them. Application forms make sure you get the information you need for a clearer evaluation of applicants and a better comparison with other prospective employees. While resumes may provide more in depth looks on applicants, they may lack specific information you might need to decide whether or not to hire someone. The application form can also serve as binding agreements for applicants to deliver what they report to deliver when you hire them. Application forms are signed for accuracy of information and you can use them to fire a person that doesn't deliver as promised on the signed form. Application forms can also serve verification purposes to ensure that data from resumes are accurate and consistent.

The interview is perhaps the most crucial part of the hiring process as it has the biggest weight for your final decision. It is important to know that the interview may not be as accurate in predicting the actual performance of an employee as you might hope. There are applicants who shine in interviews with their speaking skills and confidence but don't necessarily relate well with customers or stay loyal to you. Charisma can influence you and you should see through the veil of charm. To do this, you should ask questions that give you more objective information about the person. Ask about their interests and their backgrounds. Ask for specific incidents that give actual information about them. By the way they tell their experiences and interests, you may be able to see how they would relate with your customers. Though hypothetical questions will give you a glimpse as how creative the applicant may be, they aren't actual incidents that will accurately predict the applicant's behavior. You should also ask what the applicant's expectations for the job are. This would show if the applicants understand the line of work well enough for you to consider hiring them.

You shouldn't make the decision to hire right away. Give yourself time after the interviews before offering the job to anyone. It is important to consider all applicants and evaluate all their qualities and skills to come up with a decision. You should come up with a short list of at least five people ranked according to your preference since you can't expect everyone to grab your offer immediately.

It is important to hire a good staff for any restaurant. With careful planning of job requirements and a payment system, plus thorough selection of applicants you are at least halfway to having a successful restaurant. Cheers!

Preparing a business and financial plan

Doing the Math in the Restaurant Business: Preparing a Business and Financial Plan

Most aspirants of the restaurant business get excited with the hustle and bustle of the kitchen. Beginning restaurant entrepreneurs brace themselves for the clashing and banging of pots and pans and the action on the restaurant floor. However, preparing for the feats in a restaurant isn't enough, many who attempt to start a restaurant fail to do so because they overlook another important, albeit less exciting, portion of the business, and that is the finance part. Many fail to realize that a restaurant is after all a business, which requires careful planning. Here is an overview of how preparing a business and financial plan is done.

A restaurant's business and financial plan is usually composed of eleven sections that cover the projected operations of a particular food service being developed.

1. Company Description – the business plan begins with an overview of the entire profile of the restaurant being developed. This section describes what business entity that will operate the particular restaurant. Necessary information such as the company's founders, assets, type is stated in this section. Supplementary information is also stated such as the company's goals and visions, the company's identity, and so on. This section would also describe what kind of restaurant is being developed, as well as its location, size, general target market and other information will provide the identity of the restaurant.

2. Industry Analysis – this section provides a general overview of the restaurant industry. Careful research is needed for this section in order to provide accurate figures regarding the past trends as well as projected performance of the industry. This section gives justification as to why developing the restaurant is a worthwhile endeavor.

3. Products and Services – this section describes what the restaurant will offer. Here, the general theme of the menu will be described. This section will also provide the prospective general production scheme, stating how the food will be prepared and how other necessary measures in the production would be carried out. The manner upon which the service will be delivered will be described here as well.

4. Market Analysis – this section describes the targeted market. This will provide the profiles of the projected customers, as well as the location where they will be coming from. This section will also include a description of the observed trends in the market, such as the population growth, and other factors that might affect the restaurant's operations.

5. The Competition – this section describes the potential competitors' profiles. Other restaurants within the area will be described. The particular restaurants that have the same target market will then be discussed furthermore. The planned competitive strategy will then be described, stating how the planned restaurant will be different from the existing ones.

6. Marketing Plans and Sales Strategies – this section the plan of action to make the restaurant thrive. A description of how the market will be penetrated will be provided here. This section will also state the channels that will be tapped for advertising and generating awareness of the restaurant. The budget allotted for the marketing strategy will also be stated.

7. Operations – this part will give the details of the operating scheme. This section will describe the restaurant's facilities and equipment. The hours of operation as well as the projected holidays will be stated as well. The employee training and other aspects of human resource management will be described. The systems and controls, food production, and other services will be expounded.

8. Management and Organization – this section will give the profiles of the managing arm of the restaurant as well as its ownership. The primary employees and key managers will be described here as well as its board of directors. The compensation and incentive scheme will be explained. The management style and structure will be further expounded.

9. Long Term Development and Exit Plans – this section will provide the goals, strategies, and milestones of the restaurant. This will also predict possibilities of expansion. Risks will be evaluated.

10. Financial Data and Projections – this section will provide the current information about the company's assets at the beginning of the restaurant's development. It will also forecast projected figures in sales, expenses, profits and so on.

11. Appendices – this will give the actual data being described in the body of the business plan. The actual menu, financial statements, declaration of assets and other important information will be included here.

Having a restaurant doesn't only entail work in the kitchen or on the floor. A restaurant is primarily a business, and the business aspect of its operations should also be emphasized.

Should you borrow?

Knowing when to borrow money or secure a loan for your new business.

There are countless problems involving money. In fact, there are many individuals and businesses that cater to those in need of financial assistance. Borrowing money however may be tricky especially with the pressure of the conditions set forth by the rules of the contracts involved. The trick is to know when to borrow and with whom to borrow money from.

There are various reasons why an individual or a company resorts to securing loans. Some of the reasons include:

- To start their restaurant business
- For cash flow
- For business expansion

Thus, the motivations behind the act of borrowing money vary; and people having these common reasons for such loans have become target markets for lending institutions.

Included below are sources of financial help:

- Banks.
- Credit Unions.
- Investors.
- Family.
- Network of connections.
- Others.

The Do's of borrowing money

1.   Do your research. Before borrowing money be sure that the interest rate is within a reasonable range.
2.   Do compare. Choose the best financial institution that will give you the best value for your money.
3.   Do consolidate your borrowing activities to one account. By doing this, managing your finances will be a whole lot easier.
4.   Do check out the contract. If you are to sign for a loan, make sure you will be able to be abide with the rules set forth by the conditions of the contract.
5.   Do avoid high interest loans.
6.   Do make sure that you can pay the loan to avoid bad credit.
7.   Do borrow if it is of utmost necessity. Make sure that you need the loan and that you are paying interest for a worthy endeavor.
8.   Do keep track of the deadline of payments to avoid additional charges or fees.

Borrowing money may be scary at first because of the risks involved. However, if you are able to invest the money well and use it to earn more money to pay your debt then it becomes a calculated move with financial benefits. This is why the business plan, marketing analysis and other steps we have covered are so important.

Finding Investors

Funding your business may require you to apply for a loan. Otherwise, you may opt for an investor to fund your business instead. Attracting investors may be done with the use of a good business plan. After which, the problem will lie on locating investors who will be willing to invest.

There are various ways to look for investors; the easiest of which is through your personal connections. In fact, family members who are financially capable of investing are good people to start presenting your business plan. Moreover, family friends or college friends and colleagues looking for ways to make profit may be interested in your business venture.

Another way is to advertise. Finding investors with credible backgrounds are of utmost importance. These potential investors are also on the lookout for promising business concepts and they may very well be looking for something to invest on in the classifieds---where some are seen to make their need to invest known to the public. Also, some have also been able to locate investors this way. Just make sure that your investor won't end up stealing your business concept and start the business themselves.

Investors may sometimes offer more than financial help in ensuring the success of your business. This is especially true when your investor specializes in the same field or industry that your business caters to. These investors know the market very well through experience and may be able to give you sound advice on how to run the business. Also, as they invest their money in your business, they will be very concerned with the status of the business and with the return of their investment.

Borrowing money from any financial institution or any investor for that matter; requires a high sense of responsibility. It isn't something to be belittled and it should be accompanied with a competent plan to ensure payment of the loan or the return of investment.

Location, location, location

Making the cut: Choosing the right location and neighborhood for your restaurant business

Securing a business involves the mastery of the four P's of marketing: Product; Price; Place; and Promotion. Let's talk about the third P of marketing, and that is looking for a suitable "Place" or location for your new restaurant business. A badly located business may very well mean the death of the business; so it's consideration in ensuring the success of the business is non-questionable.

Before choosing a location for your restaurant, it is essential that you are able to identify the following factors:

- The type of restaurant.
- Target Market.
- Budget allocated for rent or purchase of space.
- Facilities needed in the set-up of the business.
- Proximity of business location to your place of residence.
- Amount of space needed to set-up the business.
- Local laws on property ownership, business permits, and other laws that are related to setting up your business.
- Desired characteristics of the space.
- Company objectives.
- Others

Assessing the needs of the restaurant will help you find a suitable location that will enable you to attend to those needs. Without a clear picture of how the business is to function and gain profit; making wise and calculated decisions on matters such as choosing a location will be close to impossible.

Surveying the potential location of the business

A thorough examination of the neighborhood or community surrounding the location where you plan to set-up your restaurant is vital in knowing if it is indeed a match for your business. Remember that your customers will be coming from the local community, and it is important that you have an adequate amount of people within the premises of your restaurant who will patronize your food services.

Finding out if the restaurant will thrive in a specific location is important in ensuring the success of your business. To do this, you must do the following steps in surveying the neighborhood:

1. Do a physical survey of the location. Spend time to view the people in the area. Other factors such as safety, cleanliness, and the like may also be factored in.

2. Check out the competition. Are there similar businesses established in the area? Find out the status of their business.

3. Get feedback from the people in the community. You may administer surveys in the place to be able to analyze the behavior of your target market. By doing so, you will have an idea of how your restaurant may be accepted if it is set-up in that location.

4. Determine spending activity of target market. It would be advisable to do a market study of the area where you intend to locate your restaurant. See the previous chapter on Market Analysis.

5. Foresee potential problems. If you decide to set-up the business in the said location, will there be any problems in the future?

6. Find out the limitations and restrictions of the given space. Match your requirements from the space needed to put up your restaurant with what is available and accessible with the given space or location. Are they a match?

7. Do the math! Determine the projected costs of setting up the restaurant in the desired location. Factor in the cost of rent, equipment, labor, and the like.

8. Analyze traffic flow and accessibility. Is the space accessible by foot or by means of transportation? It is important to know how your market will be able to go to your location.

Depending on the nature of your restaurant, the factors involving the decision to locate your business will also vary. Remember that what may work for one type of business may not work for another. The reason being that not all businesses function alike and not all have the same target market. Thus, these variations must be considered in making decisions regarding the restaurant business.

It really is all about finding that perfect match between your business needs and with what a locating can offer your business. Finding the right location may not be easy but it's important to ensure your business' success can't be overemphasized. Be patient and you'll soon find the most suitable area to house your business!

Restaurant Industry Long-Term Future

Ensuring the success of the restaurant industry's long-term future

If you own a restaurant or you're thinking of operating one, then planning for its long-term future is probably a big concern of yours. Just like any business, the restaurant industry is full of challenges and changes that affect of its' lifespan. To ensure its continued success, a well-thought out plan is definitely a must!

The restaurant business needs a market analysis before its set-up and during its operations in the market. The said market analysis would generally tackle various factors in the target market such as: age; gender; occupation; income; and education among others. By identifying these factors, the people running the business will have an idea on how to serve their customers and thrive in competition with other restaurants catering to the same target market. See the previous chapter for in-depth market analysis information.

To do forecasts of the restaurant industry's long term future, it is important to first analyze the current situation of the business. In fact, there is a need to study its operations and various conditions as it progressed from "Day 1" to the present. And this can only be done through assessing and updating the restaurant's business plan. This is not to be confused with the business plan you created when you were first starting up. A business plan should be updated frequently to insure that you are meeting your goals and objectives. Having a frequently updated business plan will help you chart your progress and make intelligent decisions regarding expansion or any other facet of your business.

For starters, it is best to identify the various factors involved:

1. Business summary highlights.
2. Company history.
3. Analysis of marketing strategies through the years – product, price, place, promotion.
4. Detailed comparison of competitors.

5. Complete products and services offered and its evolution to what is available at present.
6. Sales strategy and forecasts.
7. Quality assessment of management and operations.
8. Study of financial plan, records of profits and loses, and the like.
9. Others

Change is constant, and to ensure the long-term success of the restaurant industry, then changes in various areas of society have to be factored in present conditions and future forecasts. These are said to include the fluctuations in variables affecting the target market and in everything else that the business encompasses.

Moreover, a business plan that caters to the long term future of the restaurant industry must be conceptualized.

A good restaurant business plan will entail the following:

- Outline of company's goals.
- Competent understanding of the company's niche.
- Organized plan that allows room for growth.
- Incorporates changes and other societal conditions.
- Viable and realistic financial plan.
- Other pertinent data

Specific answers to the following questions must be answered by the forecasts:

1. What are the market trends in the restaurant industry?
2. How are these trends changing?
3. What is the future market trend forecast based on population growth?
4. What are the predicted characteristics of the target market in the long term future of the business?
5. How is the restaurant seen to evolve with various changes in the market?
6. What are the product and service changes seen down the road?
7. How have the competitors evolved?
8. What are the financial projections?
9. How will financial support be strengthened and maintained?

Various marketing strategies will help in ensuring the long term success of a restaurant. Many restaurants have actually implored the use of some of these marketing tools.

A. Use of In Store marketing

- Launching of products.
- Promotional items and discounts in the store.
- Posters, flyers, leaflets.
- Restaurant design

B. Use of community marketing
- Community programs and charity work.
- Promotions for locals.
- Sponsorship of local events

C. Use of Media
- Press releases in magazines and newspapers.
- Product features.
- Advertorials.
- Advertisements and commercials (if applicable and within budget)
- Celebrity testimonials and/or client testimonials.
- Billboards.
- Brand exposure through sponsorship

Aside from the above-mentioned marketing strategies; it is important to take note that the quality of products and services must be maintained and developed. In fact, to ensure long term success, there must be brand equity and a strong loyal customer base.

To recap the long and laboring process; ensuring the long term future involves updating the business plan of the restaurant industry, quality control of products and services, brand development, application of various marketing strategies, and the like.

Staying in the restaurant industry may prove to be a very satisfying and rewarding experience. On the other hand, mismanagement and incompetent analysis of the market may also lead to huge financial losses. Thus, every step taken in this competitive industry must be carefully weighed and properly implemented.